Communities at Work™

Community Rules

Making and Changing Rules and Laws in Communities

Jake Miller

The Rosen Publishing Group's
PowerKids Press™
New York

Published in 2005 by The Rosen Publishing Group, Inc.
29 East 21st Street, New York, NY 10010

Copyright © 2005 by The Rosen Publishing Group, Inc.

First Edition

Editor: Natashya Wilson
Book Design: Maria E. Melendez
Layout Design: Albert B. Hanner

Photo Credits: Cover and p. 1 © Steve Miller/AP Wide World Photo; p. 5 © Philip Gould/Corbis; p. 7 © Royalty-Free/Getty Images; p. 9 © Reuters/Corbis; p. 11 © Royalty-Free/Corbis; p. 13 © Klein Stephane/Corbis Sygma; p. 15 © Corbis; p. 17 © Bob Krist/Corbis; p.19 © J. Scott Applewhite/AP Wide World Photo; p. 21 © Tom Stewart/Corbis.

Library of Congress Cataloging-in-Publication Data

Miller, Jake, 1969–
Community rules : making and changing rules and laws in communities / Jake Miller.— 1st ed.
    p. cm. — (Communities at work)
Includes bibliographical references and index.
ISBN 1-4042-2782-2 (library binding) — ISBN 1-4042-5018-2 (pbk.)
1. Ordinances, Municipal—United States—Juvenile literature. 2. Legislation—United States—Juvenile literature. 3. Justice, Administration of—United States—Juvenile literature. I. Title. II. Series.

KF5313.M55 2005
342.73'09—dc22

2004000063

Manufactured in the United States of America

Contents

Rules and Laws

In a **community**, all different kinds of people live and work together. Not everyone can do what he or she wants all the time. To make sure that everyone in a community is treated fairly, communities need rules and laws. Rules and laws let people know what they can and cannot do.

One community rule is that cars must stop when people cross the street. Crossing guards work near schools to help students cross streets safely. They make sure that cars stop.

COMMUNITY NEWS

In some communities, rules are made by a few people and are followed by everyone else. In a family, parents make rules that their children must follow.

Setting Rules

Rules are guides that tell people what they should and should not do. Different kinds of communities have different ways of making rules. A town may get together in a big meeting and vote on rules. In a city, a state, or a country, people may **elect** leaders who make rules for the community.

Swimming pools often have the rule that children must be with an adult to swim. This rule helps to keep children safe at the pool.

Following Laws

Laws are rules that have been made **official** by elected leaders or **courts**. It is a crime not to follow a law. Communities have police officers to catch people who break laws.

People must follow both rules and laws. Sometimes people must pay a **fine** for breaking a rule. If they break a law, they may go to **jail**.

A police officer's job is to make sure that everyone follows community rules and laws. ▷

Understanding Rules and Laws

Sometimes rules and laws can be hard to understand. Two different people might read the same rule or law and disagree about what it means. A judge's job is to decide what a rule or a law means. A judge needs to understand rules and laws.

When people disagree about a law, it is a judge's job to say what the law means. The judge decides who is right.

Making Decisions

Rules and laws say the best way to do something. To make rules and laws the best they can be, everyone in the community must decide what he or she thinks is most important. Writing laws and rules is a way of finding out what values people in the community share.

At a town meeting, community members vote to decide community rules.

13

Changing Rules and Laws

The way people live changes over time. The rules and laws they follow must change, too. For example, at one time people did not drive cars. This meant people did not need rules about how to drive cars or where to park them. Today people do drive cars. Communities now have laws about driving and parking.

In Columbus, Ohio, in 1901, almost no one had a car. There were no rules or laws about how fast people could ride their horses. The first speed law was passed in 1902.

Solving Problems

Rules and laws can stop problems before they even start. For example, a community may have a rule that says anyone who litters must pay a big fine. No one wants to pay a big fine. The rule helps to keep people from littering. It also helps to keep the community clean!

At school, there may be a rule that says students must take turns with school supplies. There may be a sign-up sheet to show who is next. Rules can keep students from fighting over whose turn it is.

Citizens' Rights

All of the **citizens** of a community have rights. The rules of the community say what rights the citizens have. In a **democracy**, people have the right to vote. They can pick their leaders. They can help to decide what the rules and laws will be.

In the United States, citizens can gather near the White House, where the president lives. They can tell the president what they think about America's rules and laws.

Responsibilities

Members of a community have **responsibilities**. People in every community have to follow the rules and laws of the community. This is one of their responsibilities. Many communities also ask their members to pay **taxes** to help pay for community services.

Community members are responsible for keeping their community clean. Picking up trash is one way to help.

Rules and Laws Help Communities

People need and want different things. Rules and laws make it possible for all different kinds of people to live together. Rules and laws help people in communities know how to treat one another fairly. They help to keep people safe.

Glossary

citizens (SIH-tih-zenz) People who were born in or have a right to live in a country or other community.

community (kuh-MYOO-nih-tee) A place where people live and work together, or the people who make up such a place.

courts (KORTS) The places where people who break rules or laws are judged.

democracy (dih-MAH-kruh-see) A government that is run by the people who live under it.

elect (ee-LEKT) To pick for a job.

fine (FYN) Money that someone pays for doing something wrong.

jail (JAYL) A building where people who do a crime are locked up.

official (uh-FIH-shul) Decided by leaders in a fixed way.

responsibilities (rih-spon-sih-BIH-lih-teez) Things that a person must take care of or complete.

taxes (TAKS-ez) Money added to the price of something or paid to a government for community services.

Index

Web Sites

Due to the changing nature of Internet links, PowerKids Press has developed an online list of Web sites related to the subject of this book. This site is updated regularly. Please use this link to access the list:

www.powerkidslinks.com/caw/comrules/

24